Beyond Certification

Scott Poynton

Founder, The Forest Trust
s.poynton@tft-earth.org
+41 22 367 9440

Routledge
Taylor & Francis Group

LONDON AND NEW YORK

First published 2015 by Greenleaf Publishing Limited

Published 2017 by Routledge
2 Park Square, Milton Park, Abingdon, Oxon OX14 4RN
711 Third Avenue, New York, NY 10017, USA

Routledge is an imprint of the Taylor & Francis Group, an informa business

ISBN 978-1-910174-53-1 (pbk)

A catalogue record for this title is available from the British Library.

Page design and typesetting by Alison Rayner
Cover by Becky Chilcott

....

*&&And those who were seen dancing were thought to be insane
by those who could not hear the music.&&*

FRIEDRICH NIETZSCHE

....

Abstract

CERTIFICATION EMERGED from the 1992 Rio Earth Summit amidst great hope that we would finally begin to address the wicked environmental and social problems facing our globe. Despite a proliferation of certification schemes in twenty-five industry sectors over more than twenty years, the environmental and social ills resulting from destructive and irresponsible exploitation of natural and human resources have grown still worse.

Beyond Certification reviews the positive aspects of certification, of which there are many. But more important, it argues that we can no longer afford to gloss over its failures. It is powerfully clear we need a very different approach and set of actions to managing wicked problems like deforestation and exploitation. The book offers one alternative model, based on Values, Transparency, Transformation and Verification, and shares stories of how farsighted people in very large corporations in a number of industries have adopted this model to manage natural resources far more responsibly while also benefitting local communities. Part of the power of this model is that the companies work in partnership with an extensive network of NGOs, local communities, suppliers, and other stakeholders to effect needed change.

Beyond Certification does not claim that this VT-TV model is the only solution. Rather, it serves to show how new and seemingly radical thinking can resonate so strongly with many people and companies that it catalyzes positive change. It makes the case for our continuing

ABSTRACT

to invest more thought and proactive energy to develop still other approaches to grappling with the serious issues confronting us all, before it is too late.

....

About the Author

 **SCOTT POYNTON** graduated from the Australian National University School of Forestry in 1987. He gained practical forestry experience working in Tasmania for two years before studying a Masters of Forestry at Oxford. In 1993 he embarked on a career outside of Australia, starting with work on a reforestation project in Vietnam's Mekong Delta. He founded The Forest Trust (TFT) in 1999 and has led the organisation since. In addition to his experience in Australia, Poynton has worked in Africa, Europe, across Asia and the Americas and has a wealth of experience bringing change to a variety of industries, particularly the forest and wood, palm oil and pulp and paper sectors. He was deeply engaged in the certification movement for many years but has become a concerned and increasingly vocal critic since disengaging in 2012. He lives with his family in Switzerland.

Acknowledgments

THANKS TO NICK BELLORINI of Dō Sustainability for inviting me to write Beyond Certification and for his patience as the project unfolded. Many thanks to Whitney Watriss for exceptional editing and helping make sense of my initial draft. Thanks to Coimbra Sirica for introducing me to Whitney and for her unflagging belief. My professional colleagues inside TFT have offered great encouragement and a special word must go to everyone striving to protect people, plants and animals inside and outside certification schemes; if not for you, we couldn't speak of going beyond certification. Lastly, special thanks to my family, Barrie Oldfield, Robyn Williams, Richard St Barbe Baker, Michael Leunig and Lynton Keith Caldwell for the inspiration.

Contents

Abstract...9

About the Author 11

Acknowledgments 13

Preface 17

1   Introduction..................................23

2   Certification's Record...................27

3   Moving Beyond Certification 39
    V for Values! 39
    T for Transparency! 48
    T for Transformation! 52
    V for Verification!............................59
    That's it: VT-TV! 64

4   Between Two Worlds......................67

5   Setting Spirits Free 75

    References 83

    Notes 85

Preface

"Estragon: Nothing to be done.
Vladimir: I'm beginning to come round to that opinion. All my life
I've tried to put it from me, saying Vladimir, be reasonable, you
haven't yet tried everything. And I resumed the struggle."
FROM *WAITING FOR GODOT* BY SAMUEL BECKETT, 1949

WHAT A TASK IT'S BEEN WRITING THIS BOOK! The torture started at
the end of 2011 after I irreversibly crossed a deep, inner milestone and
decided I had to redirect my own struggle.

I'd just been to India where I visited some small-scale wood processing
factories. In each I spotted little areas set aside with a sign announcing
'FSC Wood'. The spaces were bare. 'No FSC wood?,' I enquired. 'No,
we never use FSC wood, we can't buy it. But we set these areas aside
to secure our FSC Chain of Custody certificate,' the factory managers
responded with bitter bemusement.

I had seen similar things on a much larger scale in China. Vast wood
factories awash with wood from the furthest reaches of the world, each
with its own tiny, empty and soulless set-aside areas, waiting in vain for
even the smallest stick of FSC wood. The factories maintained the mirage
because they wanted an FSC Chain of Custody certificate. Having it gave
them credibility. They could market themselves, like their competitors, as
good FSC-certified blokes and apparently credible businesses – despite
their use of all sorts of non-FSC and, it seemed, non-legal wood.

What I witnessed in India and China was a bridge too far. The deceit ailed me too terribly. My long association with the FSC has been a genuine love-hate affair. The FSC's great, positive points have long invigorated me to struggle on the rollercoaster of hope and despair. So many good people have invested so much of their lives to promoting and improving certification schemes with the original Earth Summit goals in mind. But we seem to have reached a point where we are stifling ourselves in a yearning for consensus and collaboration, an avoidance of fighting, even while we agree about the enormity of the challenges. Not surprisingly, any criticism is often taken personally – shooting at certification seems like shooting at the good guys and letting the real villains off the hook.

For me, it's not just the FSC. I have the same feelings with another certification scheme I've been involved with – the RSPO, or Roundtable for Sustainable Palm Oil, around since 2005. The new concept of roundtable, 'multi-stakeholder' certification originated at the 1992 Rio Earth Summit. Until then, discussions around sustainable use of natural resources had been beset by inextricable conflict among businesses, governments, NGOs, communities and other stakeholders, with people and the environment the great losers. Roundtable certification was conceived first and foremost as a way to transform away from unsustainable practices and into a new world where humans would consume sustainably. It was founded on the idea that people from diverse backgrounds could come together to agree on performance standards for specific industries. They could discuss and resolve challenging issues and address globally significant, pressing problems in an environmentally appropriate, socially beneficial and economically viable way. People saw it as having great potential to change the way humans interact with each other and with nature. By 1994, the FSC emerged as the first roundtable certification scheme. It was designed to promote better management of the world's forests by pulling together an energised group of social and environmental NGOs and businesses that would work together, most for the first time, to make things better.

Twenty years on we have many more certification schemes. As of January 2015 the Ecolabel Index lists 458 ecolabels in 25 industry sectors – palm oil, cocoa, coffee, marine fisheries to name a few – in 197 countries. Around two-thirds were developed in the last decade, and new ones continue to emerge. So many of the good people working to improve management of the world's natural resources have struggled on, re-doubling their already significant efforts to try everything to make certification work, to make it 'the solution'. I honour those people and respect their struggle. Yet from a personal perspective, my voyage to India and the inner journey it prompted confirmed what I had felt for a long time – certification isn't working and is, in fact, part of the problem.

Twenty years is a good span over which to review performance. We can look back and assess how effective roundtable certification has been. But I have found that to say anything negative is to some about like shooting at an ambulance. But while we keep our respectful silence, the world is going rapidly downhill. Serious water, soil and biodiversity issues abound in all corners of the globe – irrefutable facts, not conjecture. These intertwine with poverty and indigenous and community rights problems, and severe pressure on too many species, as humans appropriate more and more resources. Can the Earth cope with 9 billion people? Climate change is already overwhelming our ineffective efforts at control. Recently we learned the Western Antarctic Ice Sheet is melting irreversibly. Already at our current rate of warming we're destroying the systems that underpin our survival.

PREFACE

We need to wake up! We need better solutions fast! The fact that certification has been with us for more than 20 years and we still find ourselves accelerating toward our ultimate demise, suggests we need to do something different, and quickly. It's no longer enough to struggle on, to be reasonable. As we accelerate toward a >6 °C warming, we must open everything we do to intense scrutiny. Our descendants may die out leaving only insects because we've destroyed the chance for large mammals to survive on the planet.

So, however well-intentioned certification is, I have to ask if it is the right, the best, ambulance. Has our yearning for consensus blinded us to its failings, left us with something sub-standard? Along with celebrating its good points – and there are many – shouldn't we also have the courage to examine its *actual* performance? Might we not then be able to move more rapidly to a better place?

My purpose in writing this book is to air some of the issues I see with certification, and to get us to think innovatively and passionately about how we can move forward. The time for iterative tinkering is past. I also want to share one approach – VT-TV – that has had great success. I present it not as the best way forward, the only solution, but to provoke deep reflection and strong debate, and still more innovation and big thinking. I want to get people thinking deeply and in a way that really stretches our collective brainpower beyond where we are today. Most critically, I want to generate change. I hope this book encourages folk to open up to ideas outside the boxes created by 20 years of certification.

The book is for the already knowledgeable. It dives straight into issues assuming that readers are well-versed in certification. It offers no definitive history of all things certification. The few references I cite are expressions of my thinking based on many years of seeing certification in action. My ultimate purpose is to encourage people to think beyond the 'If not certification, then what?' lament I have heard so many times over the years, often uttered in despair. I had to end my struggle to 'fix' certification and push forward on another front, regardless of some people's strong reactions both in defence of certification and against new approaches. We desperately need strong reactions because only from the ensuing discussions do we stand a chance of innovation. We need to generate change *now* because we have so little time left.

A final note. Throughout this book I present stories of what beyond certification looks like, of how courageous people have led their companies to act with passion on deeply felt values about protecting and nurturing life on this planet. They do so not only for their generation, but also future generations of children, parents, city and forest dwellers, mammals, birds, reptiles, fish, trees, lichens, coral – the entire diversity of life on Earth. I would prefer to tell you who the companies in these stories are so that you can celebrate their achievements with them. But, as I explain later, breaking away from the pack can lead to unintended problems within the certification and companies' worlds. That is the last thing this book should do, and so in some cases I keep my silence. Their stories, however, stand on their own as hugely important and inspiring instances of creative spirit. They will still give you, as they've given me, faith that when we allow ourselves to choose to do the right thing, real, transformational change will happen at a scale that may, once again, allow life on Earth to flourish.

....

CHAPTER 1

Introduction

"And what is good, Phaedrus,
And what is not good –
Need we ask anyone to tell us these things?"
FROM *ZEN AND THE ART OF MOTORCYCLE MAINTENANCE,*
BY ROBERT M. PIRSIG, 1974

ALMOST EVERY WEEK since I agreed to write this book, something has happened that reinforces my view that certification cannot deliver the deep, transformational change we require, and that we badly need to go beyond its narrow constraints as quickly as possible. A two-day meeting I attended on ethical recruitment strongly reinforced my sense of urgency. It involved a great cross-section of folk from the business community, recruitment agencies, civil society, government and the UN, all working on migrant issues. The organisers had convened this multi-stakeholder group because they wanted our input on their new certification scheme to accredit recruitment agencies. Their hope was that a multi-stakeholder body could be set up to design and run the scheme and, through it, help transform the recruitment industry.

I was only able to attend the second day of the meeting, the focus of which was accreditation and licensing frameworks, monitoring and compliance mechanisms, and complaints procedures. I was to share TFT's experiences in helping folk comply with standards. Discussions on the first day had apparently bogged down very quickly over a draft of ten (why does it always have to be ten?) principles for ethical recruitment. Nothing was resolved; further discussion and process were required. I spent much of the morning of the second day just listening. By lunchtime I had a list of words – 'certification', 'licensing', 'accreditation', 'systems', 'standards', 'hoops', 'credibility', 'regulations', 'auditing', 'monitoring' and 'simplicity', the latter spoken as a plea that the scheme not become an unmanageable burden. These words had come up again and again as people shared their thoughts on what might be done to get the scheme up and running, to ensure it remained credible and simple. It wasn't an inspiring discussion. Quite the contrary. Everyone's dry mulling on the issue lacked any hint of the passion that had brought us all together.

Then, just before lunch, a fascinating thing happened. One of the recruitment agency guys jumped into the fray and broke ranks, broke away in fact, from the dry discussion of the past day and a half with a passionate speech about doing the right thing. 'We don't need anyone to tell us what's right or wrong, we already know!,' he almost yelled in exasperation. 'We know it's not right that these people pay recruitment agencies. We know it's not right that they have their passports taken. We know these things. They're self-evident.'

'We just need to do what's right!'

He didn't bang on the table, but he physically rose up. His words were full of emotion as he expressed with great passion what were clearly intense feelings and strongly held values around ethical recruitment. 'We have to *respect* these people! We have to *value* them, treat them as *human beings*,' he pleaded. He had something deep inside him that he really needed to get out, and nothing was going to stop him. His parting shot

– he was leaving the meeting at lunchtime – was to mention the need to 'do the right thing' at least five more times. His outburst was borne of frustration, of the need to tap back into that well of inspiration that had brought him and everyone else together, but that had so far failed to find expression.

It was terrific to see his passion burst forth. But even more incredible was to see everyone else in the room light up from his spark. The energy was palpable, extraordinary. In a frantic 30-minute burst everyone else fought to seize the moment, the opportunity, that his breakaway had created. Each and every person jumped in with their own passionate statements about 'doing the right thing'. No one mentioned the words on my list. There was nothing about certification schemes, systems, accreditation or regulation. People just spoke from their hearts about 'doing the right thing'. Instinctively we all knew what the right thing was, and now we just needed to get on with it.

Wow! Right there in a nutshell, the problem with certification. For one and a half days this group of great people, of true believers, who had come together on the common ground of a deeply held passion to do the right thing on ethical recruitment, had been anaesthetised by long, fruitless discussions on the ins, outs and intricacies of an ethical recruitment certification scheme. Those passionate people didn't *have to* build a certification scheme. They could have dreamed a different approach. But from the start they had chosen to stick with someone else's agenda. Certification is what everyone does, right? It's the thing. It's how you *control* people. So that's where the discussion had focused from the start. There was no room for creative 'what if' or 'beyond certification' thinking, no attention given to any different approach. The participants were there to tick someone else's boxes, to speak on someone else's agenda. It was only when that spark of passion re-entered the room through the red face, emotional voice and raised veins on the neck of the breakaway that the energy that drives the transformation they all prayed for became present.

What the group might have done instead is the focus of this book. It is fundamentally about harnessing the energy, passion and spark created by breakaways in those moments when they cast off the layers of control and speak only from the soul. It's about how we might use that enduring power, that extraordinary life force, to come up with a different approach beyond certification, and create real, transformational change in the way we interact with each other and with nature. It's about *just doing the right thing*.

It's a hopeful, whimsical story about a positive exploration of what might be, about a journey we might all take to a different place, if we're brave enough to reach down into our souls and touch that passion, that knowledge, that lives within us all to *just do the right thing*. It's a story about what some companies have in fact already done when they have acted according to their hearts and true beliefs, and broken away from the shackles of control imposed by certification.

CHAPTER 2

Certification's Record

❝We had also, to all the visitors who came over there, been one of the bright shining lies.❞
JOHN PAUL VANN TO A US ARMY HISTORIAN, JULY 1963, AS QUOTED IN
NEIL SHEEHAN'S *A BRIGHT SHINING LIE*

I PERSONALLY BELIEVE that certification is one of the brightest bright shining lies of the sustainability movement. I have seen the evidence too many times. Now, 20 years into certification, we have reached the point where we *must* take an honest look at certification to discover both its achievements *and* its fatal flaws. Despite the many people who declaim 'What do you mean certification has *failed*?', it is essential that we take this *hugely* important early step on a path toward change. While I prefer to focus on solutions, they only make sense if we understand where and why they're needed. I hope that some of the following review will shed light on our blind faith in all things certified, and move us toward doing the right thing – and quickly.

Come on, it's not *all* bad!!

Let me be very clear – certification is not all bad. Much has been written about its positive aspects by a variety of organisations and people. There is broad consensus around the seven positive contributions of certification schemes that I summarise below. Other people would surely add more.

They get protagonists together. The FSC brought NGOs, companies, communities, experts and other folk together to develop and agree to the first ever Principles of Forest Stewardship, a global standard that could be applied to any forest management context. It established the concept of multi-stakeholder standard setting and regular meetings to review and vote on new concepts and agree on new directions.

They have a strong foundation in democratic principles. Certification schemes embody democratic governance such that all members can voice their opinions and aspirations to the governing body and vote on standards and proposed changes to how the organisation operates. Generally participants cannot be bullied into a decision.

They establish agreed-to standards. Standards give concrete life to a consensus view of what good resource management looks like in a given industry. They are statements of what a particular group of stakeholders was able to agree to at a particular time, though they may not meet everyone's aspirations. Standards provide a framework for training programs on what good management looks like and how to achieve it.

They improve natural resource management. At certified operations certification has moved natural resource management in the right direction, helping resolve land-use conflicts, engage indigenous communities in positive resource management and foster respect and protection of their rights and resources. In some important cases, certification has demonstrated how business, community and nature interests can be reconciled.

They offer grievance procedures. Although anyone can file a grievance, for NGOs in particular the grievance procedures have been a key reason to engage. They provide an avenue of appeal that gives some leverage over companies seeking certification.

They enable companies to communicate their commitments. Before certification it was impossible to tell what any of the incredibly numerous sustainability labels meant, if anything. Now companies can use a single global label to communicate their sustainability commitments and performance to customers, shareholders and suppliers.

They help consumers connect with sustainability. Certification offers consumers a way to make informed choices for more ethical purchases.

OK, so what *is* the problem?

In the post-Second World War era, producers were heavily and often brutally exploiting the world's natural resources, with serious negative environmental and social consequences. Then along came certification, which provided unquestioned benefits and created a sense that we cannot do without it. In light of how bad things were before, it's understandable that people cling strongly to an innovation that offers such hope.

Yet for over a decade I have watched certification consistently fail to deliver industry-wide transformation, all the while becoming an industry in its own right. It is incontrovertible that the people and environment the certification schemes are supposed to protect, preserve and enhance aren't faring so well. If we are to believe all the excitement and razzle-dazzle about the sustainability that certification schemes purport to deliver, at the very least the world should be on a strong path toward improvement. Sadly, it isn't. Despite the hundreds of millions of dollars washing through the certification world, the many company representatives that sit on certification scheme and NGO boards, the money flowing into NGO partnerships and the positive communications and awards showered upon companies for their certification 'sustainability' efforts, the world is still headed in very much the wrong direction.

This strong disconnect demands attention. My own analysis is that certification schemes cannot and never will be able to deal with the growing number and diverse array of hugely difficult and extremely complex issues the world faces. In fact, our over-reliance on certification schemes is a big part of the problem. They allow people to make lots of money while smothering the critical analysis, debate and innovation that can lead to a fundamental transformation in how we interact with each other and the natural world.

So let's look at what's wrong with certification schemes.

A bedrock belief that people can't be trusted. An implicit consensus has emerged among all certification schemes that *people can't be trusted*. So for any scheme to be effective, it must require that participants tick *its* boxes and abide by *its* accreditation systems, *its* norms on how members interact, *its* guidance on what can and can't be said about the certification journey and its results. In short, it binds people within a framework of command and control. When certification schemes fail, for example when false claims are revealed, the standard response is to ratchet up the rules, tighten control procedures, because tricky people clearly are enacting clever workarounds. A 'failure/more rules' cycle means that each and every certification scheme has its own raft of controls to keep participants strictly in line. Probably most people don't even know they're buying into this misguided 'please don't think outside our boxes' attitude. Certainly they weren't thinking about its consequences – that this very belief that people can't be trusted kills any hope for the future.

Why? Because our future depends on our coming together to engage in some deep thinking and creative soul-searching to find innovative ways to address the wicked problems like deforestation and exploitation that beset us.[2] And after that, to continue working together to overcome those dragons. Meaningless abstractions? I don't think so – without that connection to core values and passion, and to like-minded colleagues, a company's commitment to stay the course will fall away quickly when the change journey gets tough, as inevitably it does. Then it's back to the deadly business as usual.

An end game of membership, not transformation. Certification schemes point to the number of members or participants at a meeting as proof of impact. Does the number of members necessarily equate to success or rigour? The reality is that many companies engage to be part of the 'sustainability pack'. They use certification as a risk management strategy, postponing change by engaging in the endless discussions that precede decisions.

A wrongheaded emphasis on pre-competitive processes. 'Sustainability' has always been conceived of as something that should be done pre-competitively. It is, after all, about everyone and everything winning and the whole world being made better. Logically, then, all the players should get together pre-competitively to work out the best way forward; they should seek processes that lift all boats together. They can't let certification be soiled by the nasty world of competition where bad things happen. But multi-stakeholder, pre-competitive certification processes are the opposite of the cut and thrust, uncomfortable real world that emboldens innovation and risk takers. They disarm the dynamic life force of human ingenuity that, when released, brings change and transformation. Competition is exactly what creates the risk that makes people feel vulnerable – which is when they feel a need to change.

A code of silence. Certification schemes have in-built mechanisms for silence. The norm is to communicate concerns behind closed doors. Going public is anathema because it undermines the scheme. This group-think kills debate and introspection.

A status akin to religion. With certification seen as the 'truth' and in-built mechanisms that silence criticism, certification has become something akin to a religion, where you're either in or out. And as with most religions, in some sectors the religion is fragmented into vehemently opposed 'churches'. In the forestry sector, the FSC and PEFC schemes compete with noteworthy vitriol. Again, the result is a stifling of introspection and innovation.

Standard setting and review processes that contribute to business as usual. In the case of standard setting, the quality of the standard depends on who is at the table during negotiation. When a party disagrees with a proposed change to business as usual, consensus rules the day, and the result is the lowest common denominator of agreement. Alternatively, if a party lobbies hard against a crucial change, the matter gets spun off to working groups, and after the ensuing endless process, typically the decision is business as usual. The process itself is not transparent, as concerns are hidden from public view. And any review of the standards reawakens strongly held positions and ignites endless negotiation and wordsmithing. Despite the impression of progress, are the members really happy?

The lie of the multi-stakeholder or collaborative claim. Look, for example, at what happens when companies are implementing the standard. They tend to work in isolation, changing their systems just enough to meet it. They pay the auditors who do their certification reviews. NGOs seldom take part in the implementation part of certification, particularly the audits, even though their deep engagement in the on-the-ground phase, when operations are transforming, is badly needed.

Excessive reliance on 'outsiders' and not on local capacity. Outside auditors are expensive, both in terms of travel to isolated locations and the additional hours they have to spend because they don't know the locale. That latter point is even more paramount because it also means auditing, by its very nature, involves judgement calls based on insufficient knowledge. In contrast, local civil society offers in-depth knowledge and can work faster and therefore at less cost. The rub is that local capacity to conduct audits is way too limited. Think what might have happened had we invested in local capacity building the millions we paid to outside auditors!

The disconnect between words and practice – the terrible dark side. For many critics, the worst problem is issuance of certificates to companies that don't merit them and that lower the bar. No one spots the disconnect between words and practice. Certification has become a global money-making racket that, in the pursuit of income and brand domination, compromises values.

My personal bugbear is Chain of Custody (COC), traceability certification. Effective COC should secure traceability back to source, not just within a factory complex. In reality, taking FSC COC certification as an example, this isn't what happens. FSC accredited certification bodies (CBs) certify wood processing factories for COC without verifying the origin of that wood. All they are really verifying is that the factory was COC compliant on the day of their visit. Well-prepared factories make sure they have what they need on that day and thereafter return to their normal 'no traceability' production. The same happens with social compliance audits. Another problem is that many companies shop around for the CB that charges the least for COC certification. How can they charge less? By doing less, cutting corners, using junior auditors.

In effect, then, there really is no *third party, independent auditing* in certification, independent meaning no direct economic relationship between CB and company. Rather, certification is permeated with deep conflicts of interest.

Nor is this the end. The FSC itself reaps a lot of income from the fees charged by CBs. A large training sector makes money off SMEs seeking certification. NGOs are part of this, urging companies to get certification and pushing their own workshops because this metric justifies further funding. Consumers end up unknowingly buying what are in fact non-compliant products.

A foundation of sustainability myths. One myth is that *certification equals sustainability* because a multi-stakeholder group defined a standard for sustainability within an industry. But the mere fact that a group of people agreed to a standard doesn't make it a good one or mean it will lead to sustainability.

A second myth is that *being certified means a company is sustainable*. Being certified just means that someone believed the company met the standard. But some companies fail to match their marketing spin. Often they innovate only enough to tick the certification boxes. Then they celebrate their accomplishment, and others reward them for the act of collaboration, of participation – rather than for real transformation.

A third myth is that *certification means continued sustainability and improvement*. Quite the opposite. If large NGOs and others hail a company as a sustainability hero for becoming certified, what incentive is there for the company to engage the brain further, think creatively, go beyond the standard and *innovate, transform*?

High costs and unclear benefits. Certification can add significantly to the cost burden of certified companies, but rarely do companies engage in fruitful discussion with buyers about higher prices. Even when the supply of certified material is significant, the cost still deters buyers. This is one reason only the top 10% of companies go for certification. Nor do the schemes help smallholders – cost constraints preclude them from entering the supply chains demanding certified products. If they do get certified, it is almost always because an outside source helped, and usually the cost of that help is unsustainable.

Inherent support for inaction. Companies hide behind the certification schemes and, more particularly, the NGOs that support them. Companies don't have to say what they truly believe, to truly 'own' their values. Rather, they outsource their values to the certification schemes. So long as the big NGOs say it is good, it must be good, right? But what about the quality of what the companies deliver on their promises? They also outsource that – to the certification bodies, auditors, consultants, the whole show that determines whether their products are or aren't okay. When a company is focused on ticking someone else's boxes, it doesn't have to pay attention to larger issues or to transformation. It changes only to the degree proscribed by the standard. And once certified, it doesn't *have to* address any issue not in the standard. Should there be flagrant breaches, the companies can always blame the certification schemes and tell journalists and customers that they're working with the scheme to fix their practices.

The unspoken question of opportunity cost. As if all this weren't bad enough, consider the opportunity cost of certification – what all the money pouring into certification could have been used for. New and better machinery? Improved worker health and safety? Local capacity building? Assistance to SMEs? Support for smallholder growers? Investment upstream to improve stewardship of the forests supplying raw materials? I believe the opportunity cost is in the billions of dollars.

And by far the worst of all ...

The stifling of deep, sector-wide transformation. Certification has proved an abject failure in achieving deep, sector-wide transformation, its founding goal. Certification schemes rarely affect more than 10% of any industry in which they operate. Yes, the biggest and best managers achieve certification quickly; they kick-start 'certified' trade to create an impression of success, hope and momentum. Then, as certification schemes move beyond the leaders to more complex, difficult operations, they run out of steam. Transforming a whole industry is a very different matter.

I believe the reason for this failure is that the systems, processes and command/control approaches of certification are the polar opposite of what is needed to tackle wicked problems. It's not certification's fault it has failed – we're asking it to do something that it's fundamentally incapable of doing. We've built the wrong tool. At the same time, certification insidiously gives people the impression that an effective system is in place, so they don't need to worry. It's easy to be concerned about forest destruction for example, but not many people are interested in the limitations of a certification scheme to fix the problem. If they do take an interest, then cynicism will be their likely reaction, which is as bad as indifference.

Why does all this matter, and matter a great deal? Because the whole certification approach is fuelling a destructive race to the bottom.

CHAPTER 3

Moving Beyond Certification

❝God help us to change. To change ourselves and to change our world. To know the need for it. To deal with the pain of it. To feel the joy of it. To undertake the journey without understanding the destination. The art of gentle revolution.❞
FROM *A COMMON PRAYER*, BY MICHAEL LEUNIG, 1990

WHAT DOES BEYOND CERTIFICATION LOOK LIKE? At TFT we're implementing an alternative approach with quite some success. We call it VT-TV – Values, Transparency, Transformation and Verification. VT-TV is all about change and deep transformation at scale. Just what the doctor ordered.

V for Values!

It was 19 May 2010, and I'd just arrived at Nestlé headquarters in Vevey, Switzerland. I entered the huge imposing building on the shores of Lac Leman. There, multitudes work across all aspects of the company's global business. In the entrance – a vast open, light-filled space with grand glass windows giving onto beautiful views of manicured lawns and the lake and mountains beyond – a receptionist waits to greet all visitors.

'Bonjour, good morning, your name please?,' she asked me with great politeness, a friendly smile and tidy Swiss efficiency.

'Scott Poynton,' I responded.

'And which organisation are you from, Mr. Poynton?,' came the reply.

'TFT,' I smiled back, only to note a raised eyebrow, a 'more information please' expression. 'Sorry, The Forest Trust,' I expanded, getting it that few know us by our acronym.

'Oh!! The *Forest Trust*! Thank *goodness* you're here. We're so happy to be working with you. We don't want to kill Orang-utans. That's not who we are.'

'Whoa!' I thought, almost knocked back by the power of her statement that 'We don't want to kill Orang-utans. That's not who we are.' Not the standard greeting for most visitors, I suspected, and certainly one that completely surprised me.

'Well, I'm happy to be working with you,' I responded, after taking a moment to recover.

She went on: 'Our partnership with you was announced on our intranet system two days ago, and it was a huge relief to everyone because the Greenpeace campaign really affected us. We're so pleased to be addressing the issues. Thank you.'

'Well, thank you.' I took my badge and waited, scratching my head, as she called up to let folks know I'd arrived.

The power of Values to transform

After my encounter with the receptionist, I concluded I must be dealing with an interesting organisation and that perhaps we really could turn things around. Not because of Nestlé's pledge to follow a certification scheme, but because, in the true spirit of the breakaway, the organisation *as a whole* was saying 'This is not who we are.' Values based on passion and the power of the breakaway are transformative, especially if many people hold them and are prepared to act to ensure they're not compromised.

If something is 'not who you are', you have a far lower tolerance to accept it. Indeed, you abhor it, seek to rid yourself, your whole life, of it. I personally feel that way about smoking. I choose not to smoke, I seek places where smoking is not allowed, and I try to convince my kids they shouldn't smoke. It's anathema to me when people on restaurant terraces smoke, especially when my kids are present. 'I don't like smoking' is a Values statement that guides my behaviour.

There are many such examples. Deforestation is one. I don't like it either and don't want to be linked to it. I want it to stop, and I'm not alone. More and more folk are worried about deforestation because of its link to climate change and its impacts on affected communities and species loss. The destruction is so great and has gone on for so long that people are coming to believe we're getting to the end game for many of the world's wonderful forests, and the people and biodiversity they support.

What about exploitation? All over the world, but particularly in tropical, developing countries, people are kicked off their ancestral lands to make way for large-scale agriculture, petroleum production, mining, whatever. Do we feel good about that? Is that how we want the food to arrive at our supermarkets, our tables? Do we want cars and planes fuelled by exploitation?

What about child labour? Fancy giving your kids chocolate or clothes produced by child labourers? What about labour practices in general? All sorts of things are produced by workers who are being treated like slaves or bonded labour, endure unsafe working conditions that cause death or, like we discussed in our ethical recruitment meeting, have their passports withheld.

What about poisonous chemicals? Fancy wearing shoes whose red dye poisoned the river outside the factory, even poisoned people?

Generally, the answer to these sorts of questions is a resounding 'NO!' People don't spend a long time coming up with that answer; they don't need a university education or training course. They just know it's wrong. Of course they don't want any link to child labour, human exploitation, poisoned rivers, deforestation, the extinction of iconic or even unknown species so they have a product to buy. They wonder why you even ask. They feel passionately that that is 'not who they are'.

Every product we buy and use has a story, but for many years the intricacies and entanglements of supply chains have hidden the stories. Now the information is becoming more visible through social media and the work of civil society, and as a result there is more and more concern about where products come from and their effects on the environment and people's lives. It is far easier for us, as individuals or as society as a whole, to get the true story of where the products we are thinking of buying come from. We are better able to tell if a product's story aligns with our fundamental values. If we feel strongly enough about something, we will act on it, and our actions will drive change.

Just as we do, companies also have the power to produce and shape a product in accordance with their Values, or at least those of their customers. If they don't want child labour in their products, they can ensure none is there. The same with deforestation. It's that simple. It's a cop out and abrogation of responsibility to fall back on 'But we don't know where the raw material comes from.' If they care enough, they'll find a way to know, because not knowing means a fundamental value is being compromised, is 'not who they are'.

Over the years I've experienced what happens when passions become inflamed by deeply held Values. Here are some stories about companies doing the right thing because of their values.

- ScanCom, a Danish garden furniture maker, was highlighted by the UK NGO Global Witness for using illegally sourced wood from Cambodia that was linked to human rights and environmental abuses. In response and with the help of TFT, ScanCom prepared an Environmental Policy that clearly stated its Values, who it was. One part of the policy stated that ScanCom would exclude illegal wood from all its products. Quite simply, using illegal wood was not who the company was.

- In Indonesia, the incoming President of a forest company was deeply disturbed to learn its Forest Rangers carried guns and regularly shot and killed people they deemed to be illegal loggers. Illegal loggers or otherwise, the victims were community members, fathers, husbands and sons, and their deaths were a tragedy. For the new President, killing poor community members was very definitely 'not who we are'. She had the company embark on a program called 'Drop the Gun'. It took some time, but eventually all Forest Rangers' guns were removed from company forests. The company also instituted benefit sharing to encourage local communities to protect the forests instead of logging them, leading to a great improvement in relations.

- When NGOs charged a forest management company with being a criminal destroyer of forests, the charge led it to pursue FSC certification (see box **The Start of One Company's Journey** opposite).

- The Chairman of Wilmar International, a global palm oil company, took action after his company was accused of links to fires in Sumatra that caused a choking haze across SE Asia. He knew burning forests and choking people weren't what he and his company were, and couldn't ignore the accusations. He not only committed to stopping the practice, but followed up with the most far-reaching set of policies the palm oil industry had ever seen.

- In Singapore, a global hotel brand dropped shark fin soup from its menus worldwide because the owner's children were dismayed by the treatment of sharks.

In all these cases (and many more), the power for change came from within, from deeply held values that had in some way been questioned or challenged. The overriding feeling that resulted, as with the breakaway in the ethical recruitment meeting, was a passionate 'This is not who we are!' That exasperation in turn triggered very serious and determined action. Yes, in some cases the action was a pursuit of certification to verify where the companies were on their journey. But the motivation was not certification for its own sake, but an intense and deep felt need to do the right thing.

The Start of One Company's Journey

The children of the President of a very large forest management company came home from school one evening with questions for their father. Their local paper had run stories about their father's company after an NGO had staged a campaign "event" at one of the company's local customers. The children were asked by school friends, "Doesn't your father work in the timber business?" The President's wife was confronted in a more direct, confrontational manner, "Is it true that your husband's company and your husband in particular is involved in destroying tropical rainforest?" That evening at the dinner table, the family engaged in some very challenging discussions. The President committed himself to verifying to his family – not initially to the wider world – that his company was actually protecting forests and wildlife and helping people. In his heart he truly believed it was, because those were his Values, and surely they must be manifest in the way he ran the company and how the company managed the forests.

But he found he couldn't prove it, which led him to pledge to get FSC certification. The first step was a Forest Management Policy Statement clearly setting out the company's Values, what it believed was the right way to operate. The statement became the company's guiding principles, and the FSC process became the means to verify whether the company was managing its forests accordingly.

The power of 'open source standards'

Let's return to Nestlé for a moment. In November 2009, months before Greenpeace launched its KitKat campaign, Nestlé's Chairman had strongly stated in a public presentation that the company wanted no link to deforestation in any of its products. Nestlé hadn't worked out what that meant in actual practice, how to operationalise that commitment, and needed to put meat on the bone, to be able to say to its suppliers 'Here are our specifications; please provide raw materials that meet them.'

Converting its deeply held Values into a simple but exact and powerful policy statement was not, however, Nestlé's expertise, so it reached out to people who had that expertise in the deforestation area – TFT and Greenpeace. Both provided advice and helped Nestlé figure out how to source palm oil, pulp and paper and other raw materials that didn't cause deforestation. Together we decided this meant the raw materials had to be produced legally while protecting the rights of local and indigenous communities, High Conservation Value (HVC) forests, High Carbon Stock (HCS) forests and peatlands. Voilà – in May 2010 Nestlé issued its No Deforestation Responsible Sourcing Guidelines (RSGs)! Nestlé's Value – we don't want to be linked to deforestation – had become its guideline. Since then Nestlé has gone even further, applying the RSGs to a wide range of other commodities.

Throughout this transformation Nestlé spoke with many experts, NGOs, academics and others on a wide range of topics linked to various commodities. TFT calls this process 'open source standards'. As companies work to develop policy statements that derive from their Values, they search broadly for information from sources such as experts, trusted allies, protagonists and the literature to understand current thinking and where the company can go beyond the here and now. At TFT we've often seen companies go well beyond current thinking because it wasn't ambitious enough, wasn't sufficient to help the companies live their Values. It's a hugely exciting and invigorating process because people, sometimes for the very first time, are tapping into what they truly believe. They become genuine 'breakaways', whose passion drives them to create the basis for grand change within their own businesses – and within all the businesses with which they interact! These companies use the open source approach to hear what experts are saying and recommend, and then push that advice through their own internal system to develop their own language, approach, policy statement, standards.

This genuinely multi-stakeholder, multi-source process is so powerful and liberating because the company as a whole is in control, has complete freedom. It isn't outsourcing its Values to anyone else. It's not asking anyone to tell it what to commit to. It can choose to ask as many stakeholders as it wishes, not just those sitting around a table. It can check the Internet to canvass opinion all over the world and look at others' standards and benchmark its thinking rapidly and easily. Or it can do none of this.

The open source process requires deep reflection and, for company leaders, a really in-depth look inside themselves to touch who they really are, what they, at their deepest core, believe in. There is power and profound joy in that. And what follows from that is key. The Chairman or CEO, a core team and all the staff then put together a policy, standard, guideline for the company that they own totally. They made it, and, from our experience, they are always very proud of it. This ownership carries immense power to guide actions and behaviour.

Sure, not all open source standards are great. The company may have received poor advice, or perhaps the leaders' inner values aren't what they could have been. Maybe it received great advice but chose not to go far enough with it. Whatever, the essential point is that the standards resulted from companies looking inside themselves to understand who the company really is, *and* seeking guidance from others, and then applying their own internal metric to the advice. And if they didn't go far enough, NGOs, communities and customers are there to challenge them to go further. If the resulting policy is weak, little more than greenwashing, the whole world will see it and can reject it for what it is.

The other great thing about this process is that it can evolve and change quickly because of the big-time transparent feedback loops. Both good and poor policies will get rapid feedback on which companies can act fast – they're used to making rapid decisions – so policies and standards can improve in short order. The result can be a race to the top.

T for Transparency!

'We don't have illegal wood in any of our products. That's not who we are.' I have heard that from every retailer I've spoken to since founding TFT in 1999. But how do they know, given that no one verifies it? Too good to be true? It was. When TFT started checking documents and factories in 1999, what we found was ugly. Pretty much all furniture was being made with illegal wood. Shipping documents passed through a tiny island – Labuan, off the coast of Sabah – where the logs were legalised and given a Labuan Chinese Chamber of Commerce certificate of origin. If you asked a, say, Vietnamese factory manager where his wood came from, he'd thrust those documents at you.

We find this disconnect between Values and reality *all the time*. Take this disconcerting case from 2007. A supermarket chain asked TFT to investigate the soy imported into Europe for animal feed, in this case for chickens. The company was certain, proud even, that it had no link to any deforestation whatsoever, that its chicken feed suppliers were great people and wouldn't be involved in such things. It was indignant at any suggestion to the contrary.

Well, a five-minute scratch of the surface revealed a very disturbing counter-reality. We found that all the soy came from the Amazon, then a big driver of deforestation. Another very troublesome finding was that 80% of the soy was GMO, genetically modified organisms. This deeply shocked the supermarket chain because Europeans *really don't like* GMOs. Using GMOs in Europe is a big-time 'not who we are'. The supermarket directors' terror at what might happen if their customers learned about the GMO soy overwhelmed any concern about deforestation.

These kinds of disconnects are frighteningly common.

How might a company avoid this situation? Well, it's feeling pretty good because it produced a statement of Values, what it fundamentally believes in and is proud of. Good on it! It puts the statement on its website, shares it broadly internally. Staff feel good about it, as does the Board. The company's also shared the Values statement with NGOs, experts, customers, suppliers, stakeholders. Great! But, gulp . . . now it has to implement its policy, its Values. In our VT-TV approach, here is where it gets scary, because the first step of implementation is Transparency – within the company and with stakeholders. It means the company has to *know* if it is doing something contrary to its new Values statement, its policy, such as where its raw materials come from.

Transparency begins with 'Traceability', or mapping the supply chain to a raw material source. Likely a company knows its Tier 1 supplier(s), the ones it buys from directly. But often it has no idea who the Tier 2 suppliers are that Tier 1 buys from. Traceability back to Tiers 3, 4 and possibly beyond is even murkier. The mapping can be really hard in cases such as palm oil derivatives. But TFT believes a company can find a way to track *every* raw material to its source if it cares deeply enough about its Values. Saying 'We don't know where our raw materials come from' really means 'We don't care.'

Once a company has developed its supply map, even one with holes, the next task is to share it. While scary, this 'radical transparency' is critical because it opens up all sorts of opportunities for the company. Foremost, it shows stakeholders the company isn't hiding anything. This is something of a revolution, because NGOs tend to assume companies are 'shady', that they don't like to collaborate and share information, that they're more likely than not hiding bad things about their operations that would embarrass them if made public. Sharing something hitherto considered highly confidential, of being open and transparent, has a power that cannot be overstated. The whole discussion with antagonistic NGOs changes when they know a company is prepared to share information. At the very least they will *engage in*, even become deeply *involved in*, a dialogue.

The importance of this shift is that it moves the concept of 'multi-stakeholder engagement' beyond standard-setting into standard *imple-mentation*. It's hugely powerful. And so long as the NGOs keep the shared information confidential, and from our experience they generally do, it is possible for trust, a crucial ingredient in any change process, to grow. With trust comes more and deeper dialogue and discussions that can focus on really tough issues, on solving truly wicked problems. People genuinely start to *work together* – very revolutionary indeed!

A very few companies have gone so far as to make their supplier lists completely transparent. Why? If NGOs, experts or concerned citizens know who the suppliers are, they can provide invaluable insights into the quality of suppliers' operations, good and bad. For sure a company might learn that some of its supply base is doing things contrary to its values. But equally it might learn of suppliers that are doing great, that are just as committed to the same issues and well advanced in doing something about them. Great news for sure! There might be still others that have just embarked on a journey to address the issues. Bottom line is, the company gets to know all this information. Armed with the information, it can make better informed decisions. As to the reason companies give for not divulging their supplier lists – competitors will take their suppliers away – TFT's experience is that that doesn't happen. This knowledge will in turn lead more companies to pursue this area of Transparency.

Another benefit. The dialogue about what a company is and should be doing is far less stressful than when there's conflict. Better to have someone in your Boardroom than hanging off your building or running around your store dressed as an orang-utan, tiger or other endangered species. Better to be speaking with people than having them attack you on the Internet, TV or in the daily papers. Talking to protagonists might be stressful at first, but if handled well, trust and partnership quickly emerge because few NGOs seek to put companies out of business. They're worried about an issue that, if they were to let themselves think about it, companies worry about too.

So Transparency gets companies underway. They now know about their suppliers, or if they don't, they know how to get the information. They know where the issues are and can start addressing them. With all that knowledge, it's time for them to act.

T for Transformation!

Core to the VT-TV approach, and what TFT recommends, is Transformation. It's all about grappling with those truly wicked problems that defy simple solutions. It's about changing behaviours – the company's and others' – through deep introspection, trial and error, discussions, adaptive leadership, learning and innovation. While it's generally very gruelling work, it is also the start of a hugely fulfilling journey of real responsible action, of grappling with new challenges, of highs and lows, successes and failures. The company chooses the journey because of its deep commitment to the pursuit of its Values. Transformation is by far the hardest part of VT-TV, but in many ways the most fulfilling. (See box **The ScanCom Transformation Story** on page 57.)

The Transformation journey is never-ending. It can take years to go from nowhere to achieving an ambitious set of Values (a TFT member once described the Transformation process as starting on a moped but eventually driving an F1 car). As the journey unfolds, new journeys start, new Values are added as new information comes to light, say, about a business practice that hadn't been understood previously, or about new positive ways of acting. All the time stronger bonds are forming between suppliers and buyers. The continuous nature of the journey is a priceless and important part of the VT-TV model.

Why is this Transformation step so difficult, so very difficult? For one, when most companies start the VT-TV journey, they are nowhere near where they want to be. Massive challenges confront them as they try to move forward. Here's one of those challenges. Suppose a company learns through the Transparency process that almost none, maybe none at all, of its suppliers align with its Values. It could decide at this junction that the challenge is too great and give up. But TFT's experience is that by the time companies get to this point, most are so motivated they choose to forge ahead. Another option is to cut out all the suppliers that don't meet the company's Values. Not so easy or even desirable. Most suppliers, until challenged, have not had any reason to consider the company's new Values. And it costs suppliers a lot more to use the legal or, worse, 'sustainable' raw material. Yet here come these companies with their sparkling new Values statements asking suppliers to use this more costly raw material at the same time they're telling them to reduce their costs another 10%. The companies have already screwed down what they will pay so tightly that the suppliers have had to cut corners to survive. Not surprising that they use illegal wood, and don't pay their workers a fair wage and provide health benefits and safety stuff.

There's no 'step-by-step' process to Transformation, to dealing with these very knotty challenges. Every company will have a different approach. Still, the elements of the journey are essentially the same. Here are three of the most important.

Getting help

Having found out about its issues during the Transparency stage, the company needs to set about fixing them. Again, how to do so might not be within its area of expertise. After all, it buys palm oil and sells confectionary – what does it know about deforestation, illegal logging, indigenous peoples' rights? Here again, its new found trust and relationships with NGOs, experts and other stakeholders come to the fore. The company might choose to work with some of them or might ask for referrals to other experts. It might choose to hire someone with the required expertise to bring that knowledge and capability into the company. The new partners can advise on good candidates.

Bringing suppliers on board

Key to Transformation is changing the company's relationship with its suppliers, bringing them on board. How to do that? Many factors come into play.

Appeal to their values. Factories, lumber companies, plantation owners, mining companies, etc. also have Values, and surprisingly perhaps, they are generally pretty close to those of the rest of us. A fundamental assumption of the VT-TV model is that few people are evil and that, quite the contrary, just about everyone can be genuine and powerful forces for good. A company's supply chain partners have children and grandchildren, and they worry for their futures. One way to engage suppliers in a new and long-term partnership, then, is to appeal to their core Values and how those can guide a new way of operating. Suppliers don't wake up wondering 'how many orang-utans can I kill today?' These negative things happen as a consequence of the business model industries follow, not because of evil residing deep in their hearts. Companies can change their business models, and that is the point of deep engagement with suppliers in this Transformation phase.

The strength of loyalty. Companies sometimes have long-term relation-ships with suppliers, and just dropping them isn't a happy thing for either side. Letting suppliers know the company might be forced to do so if the suppliers can't meet the new Values generally makes them ponder how they might change to deliver what's needed.

Logistics. Just up and moving a supply base isn't straightforward. Buyers buy from factories or regions for several reasons – low prices, good products, easy shipping. Again, it's hard to let all that go.

Brand. Sometimes it just isn't important whether a respected company buys a small or large proportion of its products from a single factory. To that supplier, being able to go to the bank, to colleagues, to family members and proudly state that 'Company XXX' is a customer can be hugely important. A supplier wants to safeguard that 'face'.

In short, there are many factors that influence this question of leverage. We've been continually surprised at how suppliers really hate losing a single customer, large or small, and will generally bend over backwards to protect their business. If that means developing their own sourcing policy and implementing it parallel with the company's and their own values, with the company's support and even capacity building, that's a real win for both of them – and for the issue the company's concerned about. Excellent!

Indeed, a major benefit of this Transformation process is that supply chain partnerships become very much stronger. Buyers come to suppliers with an ask that goes way beyond the normal discussions around price, technical quality specifications and delivery schedules. 'We need to be sure the palm oil isn't linked to deforestation' or 'It's important to us that the conditions for workers in the factory are world class.' The list goes on, and it's getting longer as more issues come to light. By engaging and pledging to work together to find solutions, buyers and suppliers become more entwined. They learn things about each other as the journey toward achieving the values unfolds. They go through tough times and discussions. As they emerge on the other side and things are working, change starts to happen, and they share in celebrating their success. There is real value here.

Sharing the Transformation journey

Over time, as the company learns and its projects and programs unfold, bringing change, training, capacity building, new partnerships, new agreements, it needs to remember the other T – Transparency – and report on its progress at regular intervals. Open, honest and transparent (there's that word again) communication is important to the whole VT-TV process. The purpose is not to impress with successes, but to engage in honest, truthful reflection about the entire process, good and bad – although sharing successes is a great thing to do. A company's report should factually share how it is progressing, talk about the issues and challenges, how it deals with them and what has worked. As the company progresses from the shock of finding that it's nowhere near where it wants to be, to gradual and then accelerated improvement, it's important to tell the story. It can be told through facts and figures – xx% of its products now meet this value, yy% meet this other one, and here's its action plan to change the rest.

But it's equally important to share the story through narratives that describe how the company's actions are changing people's lives, improving the environment, the true change stories. These stories are so important because they are what engage people's minds and pull them into the journey. They inspire understanding and belief that change is possible. This is critical, because beyond achieving its goals for itself, the company wants to inspire and help others along their path. And the task of getting suppliers to move is easier if more than one company is asking them to change.

The ScanCom Transformation Story

When Danish furniture maker ScanCom started on its journey to exclude illegal wood from its products back in 1998, it was this 'acting' part that totally transformed not just its business, but also the entire wooden garden furniture sector. In this 'acting' part ScanCom learned about shipping, about establishing traceability COC systems in suppliers' factories, about the FSC and its accredited auditors, about a new marketing approach, about how to strengthen its engagement with NGOs by listening to their concerns and deeply understand everything that was happening in its business. Having learned these things about its wood operations, it applied the same principles to other parts of its business. It was a genuine journey of discovery and innovation, unlocked by the power inherent in the pursuit of its Values.

ScanCom needed a significant amount of wood to make its products, but under its new Environmental Policy it wanted to know exactly where the wood came from, and it wanted the wood to meet its Values. So it began by setting out to understand in what ways its operations weren't aligned with its policy and Values – the Transparency part. What it found wasn't good. It really had no idea where its wood came from, and, worse, no amount of discussion with its suppliers led it to believe they could change that. At that time the wood market across SE Asia was built for opacity. Illegal wood was the norm, and the many traders and middlemen who profited from its sale weren't remotely interested in changing their behaviour.

When it was clear that no one in the region could supply the wood and deliver on ScanCom's policy and Values, the company decided to buy the wood itself. It established a wood procurement team to purchase and bring the supply it needed to its Vietnamese suppliers. The team scoured the globe for wood sources that could meet its Values. First, it found FSC certified Meranti timber in Sabah, Malaysia, and brought the first ever shipment of any FSC certified wood to Vietnam. Then it found FSC certified *Eucalyptus deglupta* plantation wood in the Solomon Islands. ScanCom's Vietnamese suppliers, attuned to the magnificent, huge, dense, cylindrical illegal logs that came from natural forest, at first refused to buy the small, light, plantation grown Eucalyptus from the Solomons. This was an important crossroads because the timber was available in volume, unlike the Meranti from Sabah, and represented a great opportunity. ScanCom persuaded three factories to take a chance. Albeit with gritted teeth, the three moved ahead, and the first FSC Eucalyptus chairs ever in Vietnam rolled off their production lines. A new industry was born! ScanCom then found and brought FSC Eucalyptus timber from both South Africa and Brazil.

ScanCom had transformed itself. But equally important was that its transformation sparked a transformation in the entire wooden garden furniture industry. Upon seeing ScanCom's success with the new wood, the other companies started racing to catch up. Within a very short period, all were committed to using FSC-certified Eucalyptus timber.

Many elements were involved in ScanCom's transformation. But at its core the journey started with the NGO campaigns against the company's use of illegal wood and its heartfelt decision to commit to operating in accordance with its own environmental Values and to interact in a transparent and collaborative manner with people on the outside, to use their experience and advice on how to grapple with the tough problems the company faced in acting on its Values.

V for Verification!

As the journey unfolds, a company needs to know how it's doing. While positive feedback is good, the most useful is on where to improve. The company's suppliers, NGO partners, consultants, expert advisors or others with close links can provide that information. By asking people to check where it's going, the company can learn new things and get new ideas. But it's also important to get the insights of people with no conflict of interest.

We call this part Verification. Being honest, this part of our VT-TV beyond certification model is the least developed. Our focus to date has been on getting the Values, Transparency and Transformation parts right. But it's also because the tools now available for true independent verification are fundamentally flawed and limited. Here's one example. As I've said, most certification schemes call for independent third party verification,[3] but typically companies pay accredited CBs – a clear conflict of interest. At TFT we believe that only truly independent verification is credible, and that can only happen when the organisation doing the work is paid independently.

The all-important grievance procedure

Central to Verification is a grievance procedure. It must involve a simple, easy to use and totally transparent (that word yet again) system by which anyone, anywhere, can lodge a complaint or 'grievance' with the company over the application of its policy.

'You said you wanted no link to deforestation, yet this supplier is chopping down forests. What's going on?'

'You said you wanted no link to child labour, but there are children working in that factory, in that farm.'

'The migrant workers here are telling friends their passports have been confiscated and they're being forced to work.'

Etc., etc., etc.

This information is massively powerful and helpful. Some companies hate getting such feedback because they feel everything is under attack – their integrity, the policy of which they are very proud, who they are. Over time, they get over the feeling of injustice, or it diminishes as they realise how incredibly useful the information is in capturing misdeeds and policy breaches.

Here is one powerful reason the information is so useful. A lot of companies have many suppliers, and checking up on all of them in great detail, is *very tough*. By opening the company up to Verification through a strong, open grievance procedure, the company taps into a huge network of locally based eyes and ears. Again, as noted under Transparency, here's where making the company's supplier list publicly available is so beneficial. By hiding that information, not only does the company look shady, but it's also cutting itself off from a completely independent force for verifying policy implementation. If the world knows where the company gets its raw materials, it can help check how the suppliers are doing against the policy. The alternative is guesses, usually semi-informed ones, based on information in the public domain that might be out of date, for example, the problem supplier no longer works with the company. But that truth doesn't matter when the supposed policy breach ends up on the front page of the paper or goes viral on social media. Then the company has to go into 'correction' mode, trying to set the record straight. (See box **TFT Verification Stories from Asia** on page 62.)

While it is very tough for companies to be so transparent with their supplier list, they come to understand, as they grapple with untruths about their operations and policy, how powerful and useful the Verification process can be. A company may not love NGOs or local communities or the information they put out, but it has to get over that and just accept the information for what it is – great intelligence – and check it out. If it's true, then it has to do something about it. Over time, as communities and NGOs realise the company acts on the information they provide, that trust we talked about earlier builds, and the company can rely on many eyes and ears to alert it to issues *before* they hit the newswires and social media. This is a hugely healthy, multi-stakeholder, independent Verification process, *free of any conflict of interest*.

The key thing to understand is that in the real world, policy and values breaches *will* happen. There's poverty, corruption, money to be made. People make genuine mistakes. So we need this Verification process and a strong but simple grievance procedure to allow the mistakes to be spotted and investigated as soon as possible. If the breach is real, then the company has to act.

TFT Verification Stories from Asia

A number of TFT members operating in Asia offer terrific examples of how well Verification can work:

- Some excellent local NGOs in Asia specialise in checking whether companies are adhering to their policies and values statements. A number of Asian based TFT members have made No Deforestation commitments and established or are going to establish simple Grievance Procedures by which anyone can bring information to them. Some have gone further than any company so far, transparently sharing their full supplier list via an online dashboard. Now local and international NGOs can check the activities of their suppliers against the companies' policies.

- New satellite technology developed by the World Resources Institute with its Global Forest Watch system allows anyone in the world to check in more or less real time whether forest cover has changed. With TFT members' transparent sharing of its suppliers' maps, boundaries can be overlaid on forest cover and NGOs can check how things are progressing. That's real independent Verification. There have been cases where local NGOs have spotted deforestation and publicly reported it. A company can undertake on-the-ground investigations alongside the NGOs to check what's happening and report its findings. It can then fix policy breaches and remedy oversights and misconceptions.

The urgent need for local Verification capacity

A significant obstacle to truly independent Verification is that few international and even fewer local NGOs have the capacity to do the audits. Local communities and NGOs are too busy with their own survival to have time to check for breaches of company policy. What happens, then, is that the companies pay CBs to conduct their audits. *Not good.* Even if local capacity were there, money to pay them for independent audits is in short supply. So capacity building and money for auditing must be priorities for true Verification.

You might say that new satellite technology can help, allowing anyone in the world to check more or less in real time on whether forest cover has changed. It further helps if a company shares its suppliers' maps, so boundaries can be overlaid on forest cover. Unfortunately, such technology is not as useful for checking on social issues, fisheries and some other natural resource sectors, or the inside of factories.

So we need a systemic approach to building local Verification capacity and money to enable us to tap into local independent expertise. Here are a few options; more will emerge as others think about this matter.

Leverage the strong tradition of foundation support to build the capacity of local NGOs. European and US-based foundations could direct more support to build capacity for local monitoring, auditing and Verification.

Have companies pay into a central Verification fund. It's not right that companies get Verification as a completely free service, because the work, though painful at times, is essential to their journey to achieving their Values. They should pay for it. One way is for them to contribute anonymously to a central fund for capacity building for local NGOs, with the funds also available to pay local communities and NGOs to do the work. This approach creates a firewall between company and verifier, with the latter having no ability to link the money from the fund to a particular company. We had a situation not so long ago where a TFT member company was supporting local NGOs to undertake Verification visits, paying for flights, hotels, food and drinks. Then one NGO asked for a fee-for-service. As soon as money enters the discussion, it may seem that the seemingly independent NGO is just after the company's money or that the transfer of a fee amounts to a bribe to go easy. At this point true independent Verification is impossible, just as it is for certification bodies.

Share the benefits from good resource management. There is much scope for fostering local Verification through innovative benefit sharing with local communities. For example, in the case of the Drop the Gun program in Indonesia, the company asked former illegal loggers to help them implement its Values. It agreed to share revenue from forest management with the communities in return for their help in monitoring the forests. Community members became community forest rangers, reporting any instances where the company's policy was being breached. This led to a huge reduction in illegal logging, much improved relationships with the communities and a company able to feel that it was really meeting its Values.

That's it: VT-TV!

You might be wondering, if that's it, what's all the fuss? Is the VT-TV model really that simple – no pages of procedures, policies, etc., etc.?

TFT's VT-TV model is a breakaway-, passion- and Values-driven effort that for the past 16 years has gone beyond certification to bring about substantive change and deep transformation. Its simplicity is deliberate.

Here's a summary of the fundamental pretexts VT-TV relies on to produce real change and deep transformation:

- A belief that people can be and are real forces for positive change.

- A belief that people on their own know deeply what's right *and* what's wrong.

- Release of the deep passion in people to do what's right, the creation of breakaways.

- A statement of the company's Values – what it is and what it believes in.

- Multi-stakeholder engagement at every step of the change journey, not just at standard-setting.

- Transparency all along the change journey.

- Judging people for how they respond to inevitable policy breaches, not for the breaches themselves.

- Working with one another to build trust, and bringing together a diverse and often divided community.

....

CHAPTER 4

Between Two Worlds

❝The crisis of our times grows out of our perverse reluctance to accept the judgment of history on the modern world, and to take up the difficult task of making the changes in attitudes, behaviors, and institutions required for the transition to an enduring and endurable future. It is a crisis of will and rationality – and its outcome remains uncertain. ❞

FROM *BETWEEN TWO WORLDS: SCIENCE, THE ENVIRONMENTAL MOVEMENT AND POLICY CHOICE*, BY LYNTON KEITH CALDWELL, 1990

NESTLÉ'S ANNOUNCEMENT OF ITS PALM OIL 'No Deforestation Responsible Sourcing Guidelines' (**www.nestle.com/media/statements/pages/update-on-deforestation-and-palm-oil.aspx**), like the 'Big Bang', set free boundless energy that continues to reverberate and expand through the global agricultural commodity markets today. Take the palm oil industry, where Nestlé's passion precipitated a deep and unprecedented transformation. GAR, the world's second largest palm oil grower, committed to No Deforestation. Wilmar International, the world's largest palm oil company, went further with No Deforestation, No Exploitation and No Peatland development policies, a new benchmark. There's now a tsunami of No Deforestation announcements and other commitments going well beyond certification. NGOs are checking to be sure the companies keep true to their word and raise red flags where they see disconnects.

What we're witnessing is a race to the top, fuelled by unconstrained creative energy that drives incredible innovation as people grapple, together, with wicked problems. How do you know if you're causing deforestation if you don't have a good definition of what that means? Good question, and people from very diverse business, NGO and scientific backgrounds have been grappling with it since Nestlé and then GAR committed to protecting HCS forests. The desire to advance the HSC forest concept has pulled people together to discuss and agree on which strata should be protected and which can be cleared, recognising, however, that ongoing research could lead to changes. A truly multi-stakeholder, open source process is now underway to define and implement the HCS concept in a diversity of contexts. The concept gets more complex as it is challenged to deal with more wicked problems.

But what about indigenous and local people, you ask? Do customary rights holders of the land in question want the forest to be cleared to create income and jobs, or want no development at all? What about government, which is supposed to help people out of poverty – how does it trade off the desire to protect forests with the development of poor communities? In some places, past land use has left a lot of degraded land where there is room to balance forest conservation with development. Protect that forest there, develop new plantations over here. But where there isn't much degraded land on which to locate plantations and meet No Deforestation commitments, what to do? In Liberia, Cameroon, PNG and West Papua, No Deforestation commitments are butting heads against government and community socio-economic development goals. Here, too, passion and innovation are being directed at these wicked problems. People's brains are hurting with the challenge.

There's more. Because traceability is extremely expensive, very few companies have been buying significant volumes of fully traceable palm oil. Now, however, some are saying 'Hold on. We've made this commitment – we don't want to be linked to deforestation.' Here, too, people have come together to *think* about solutions, pilot them and test them on the ground. People learn, and that learning drives more innovation. (See box **An Innovation in Traceability in the Wood Sector** below.)

An Innovation in Traceability in the Wood Sector

What's happening in the wood sector where TFT started back in 1999? Recall that I said the FSC COC wasn't excluding illegal wood. So TFT, in conjunction with its members, decided to innovate to address this problem. Knowing that factories can 'fix' their documents in advance of a single annual audit, we decided to build them a database system that needs input *every day* of production. That allows us to identify where they buy their wood, and get out into those forests to see what's happening, decide if it meets our members' Values. We are using TFT staff inside the factories whenever production is happening to check, re-check, triple-check and then, before any container of product can be shipped, check again. Sounds hugely expensive? It doesn't seem to be. Our members have us checking production and shipments from over 100 factories in Indonesia and Vietnam. We're confident we know exactly what wood is being used in our members' products. It can be done if you work *with* people. They know how to sneak illegal wood into a product, so they must know how to keep it out, right? If you see them as part of the solution as opposed to someone to

---

> force into compliance, you energise their inherent capacity to do good. Our approach is working.

In the past, companies wouldn't have engaged in these discussions; they'd have just come in with their legal licences and cleared the forest. Now more and more and larger and larger companies are saying 'that's not who we are' and grappling instead. They're engaging in *hugely* important and healthy discussions with NGOs, government, experts and other people. The work is tough, difficult, extremely messy. It requires trade-offs, respect, humility, listening, table-thumping, raised veins on necks, despair, exhilaration, *emotions*. But all this is *good*, because working forward together, step by step, seems to me the only possible path to resolution of the wicked problems we face.

Innovation can also be seen in new technical approaches that are emerging from company commitments not to buy deforestation, exploitation and child labour, and to help local communities become resilient in the face of growing challenges, to have self-determination. Growers, traders, refiners, buyers, NGOs and experts are working together way beyond just setting a standard. The *whole* supply chain and all the stakeholders are grappling with *implementation* challenges, with wicked problems in supply chains, with *Verification* issues, in ways never before envisaged.

This movement has been moving beyond palm oil. The HCS concept, for example, is slowly making inroads in the soy industry. Nestlé has extended and redefined its RSGs to cover 12 different commodities and a range of environmental and social issues. Companies in the pulp and paper sector have announced No Deforestation policies and are now grappling with HCS, as well as HCV, social conflict, FPIC and peatland issues. TFT's work with its partners is impacting hundreds of billions of dollars of product turnover as they struggle to figure out a huge diversity of wicked problems every day across a diversity of sectors.

The race to the top has become more extended, more intense. All this grappling by communities, NGOs, experts, governments, customers working alongside each other to unlock ever more creative thinking and innovation sets other companies to watch and wonder how they, too, can become leaders. Wow!

Asking the simple question 'What do *you* believe?', and reassuring people that that is what is most important, has been setting them free. The question helps people better understand the context in which they're operating and the consequences of their company's actions or inactions. We're moving from conflict to deep collaboration on a whole range of really difficult issues simply because of the power of the breakaway, of releasing people's inherent passion to just do the right thing.

All this progress is truly great. But we also need to take time to pause and reflect, to feel what our stomachs are telling us. Are we getting excited by this new focus on Values and the passion they set free the same way we did with certification back in the 1990s? In 20 years' time will we be looking back and saying 'Hmmph, that didn't work either?' That's a risk. Nothing about the future is certain, and there's a better than good chance we won't make the transition to an enduring and endurable future.

But I'm convinced it's a small risk and that we're in a very new space that *will* work if we just open our minds to other ways of working, just face up to the certification crisis. This process of linking people back to who they really are, and to an understanding of their deep beliefs and attitudes, is having monumental effects on how they behave. It's giving us a chance to find a way forward through the wicked problems we've created. It's giving rise to new institutions that *might* yet help us work out a way forward.

Although Caldwell's text at the start of this chapter was written in the late 1980s, few would argue that things have improved since his call to action. We are in a 'crisis of our times', and to date we've refused to accept the judgement of history on the systems we've established to deal with it. Certification hasn't succeeded, and we need to open our minds to other ways of working. Our perverse reluctance to do so, our blind and rigid faith in certification to control people and their behaviour, are holding back the creative thinking and innovation we need to deal with the awful mess we're in.

I am hopeful because I come out of tough discussions every day cele-brating that they are happening at all. I wish they weren't so tough, weren't laced with accusations. But hey, that's people, and in the past these kinds of discussions would never have happened. They would have involved NGOs telling companies why they were so evil and awful and companies telling NGOs why they were so wrong. At least the tough discussions I'm in today are focused on 'How the hell are we going to solve this bloody problem!'

Today we stand between these two different worlds. The historic, where we seek to control people through box-ticking compliance systems that have us hurtling toward a 6°C global warming. The other a possible future where we grapple *together* with the crisis we've made.

We have only this one planet, which we inhabit together with our brothers, sisters, parents, friends, enemies and people we don't know. And with a whole array of beautiful and ugly and in-between plants and animals that comprise the natural world whose systems give us life. I truly believe we can make the transition to that new future.

To do so, we will have to aggressively let go of things past. The VT-TV model is a start. We look forward to evolving and improving it alongside and in tough discussions with people everywhere, and their various beliefs, cultures and traditions. Because I don't believe a single solution exists, I equally welcome someone racing ahead and coming up with something even better. I shout to you, 'Come on people! Let's look beyond our religious adherence to certification to find something that works.' (See box **The Heart of the VT-TV Process** below.)

The Heart of the VT-TV Process

- Look deeply into your soul and determine *your* Values, what you deeply believe.

- Canvass a broad range of stakeholders and information to help translate those Values into standards.

- Share the standards internally and externally, reflect on the feedback, revise, consult again, until you are ready to finalise them into your policy statement.

- Publish and communicate your policy statement.

- Hear the feedback.

- Implement your policy statement throughout your business.

- Keep learning from your experience, from feedback and

---

from developments and emerging challenges that affect your issues.

- Act on that information. Keep changing and improving. Staying still is death.

CHAPTER 5

Setting Spirits Free

❝Nature may be wooed but not coerced. And so it is with human beings – they too must be wooed from their destructive habits and be made aware of their inward kinship with the earth and all living things.❞
FROM "LAND OF TANÉ", RICHARD ST BARBE BAKER, 1956

Deep into a 12-month change journey with the leaders of a global brand, I was travelling home from my office one evening and took a moment to reflect on a wonderful poem I had sent the company just over a year earlier, when I berated it for inaction on a set of critical issues that NGOS had raised against it. The poem, called 'Autobiography in Five Short Chapters', by Portia Nelson, describes a simple yet still challenging change journey:

....

Chapter One
I walk down the street.
There is a deep hole in the sidewalk. I fall in.
I am lost . . . I am helpless.
It isn't my fault.
It takes me forever to find a way out.

Chapter Two
I walk down the same street. There is a deep hole in the sidewalk.

I pretend I don't see it.

I fall in again.

I can't believe I am in the same place but it isn't my fault.

It still takes a long time to get out.

Chapter Three

I walk down the same street.

There is a deep hole in the sidewalk.

I see it is there. I still fall in . . . it's a habit.

My eyes are open. I know where I am.

It is my fault.

I get out immediately.

Chapter Four

I walk down the same street.

There is a deep hole in the sidewalk.

I walk around it.

Chapter Five

I walk down another street.

. . . .

I had concluded that the company was languishing at chapter 2 and told it so in no uncertain terms. I didn't feel it was taking responsibility for the challenges it was facing, or that it accepted that much of what was happening was its own fault and that it could do things differently. My accusation went down like a lead balloon, and our discussions ended forthwith.

Yet six months later the company re-engaged in our discussions, and we embarked on an ambitious change journey to grapple intensely with the issues it faced. Some months later, on that trip home from work, the poem returned to me, and I thought, 'You know, I think the company's made it to chapter 4. And it stands on the threshold of chapter 5!'

On arriving home I sat down at the computer and wrote the company a long email. I sent the poem again and reminded it of our own painful chapter when our relationship had foundered, and how I was now looking back over the journey we had since made through the lens of Nelson's chapters. The company had made various policy commitments since and the milestones it had crossed with each announcement marked, in hindsight, its passage through chapters 3 and 4. The decision it was pondering at that very moment – whether to announce a No Deforestation commitment – represented a move to chapter 5. Moving away from any link to deforestation amounted to heading down a completely different street. I told the company this, encouraged it to take the plunge, sent the email and waited.

I was to meet the company a week later. By the time I got on the train, I had had no response to my email.

When I arrived and found my way to the meeting room, the company's response was exhilarating. 'Chapter 5!' people shouted as I entered the room. 'All we've been speaking about since your email is moving to chapter 5.' The company made the policy decision and ended all sourcing links to deforestation.

Let's be clear. The poem didn't open the company's eyes to something it hadn't already been pondering. The idea of ending all links to deforestation had been pushed by NGOs for a decade and been on the company's table for two years. What the poem did was help the company's leaders see a new and different context for the decision, to understand it as a different path to the future. The poem resonated with something inside them – it was a wooing, not a coercion. Most critically, it helped them see the logic of taking the decision immediately instead of continuing to consider it for an undefined future date as they had been doing up to that point.

Something similar happened with Wilmar International, another company TFT works with. On 5 December 2013 Wilmar announced its No Deforestation, No Exploitation and No Peatland development policies. These policies created a huge tremor across the global palm oil industry. Here was the sector's largest company breaking ranks. And not only was it declaring it would implement these policies across its own plantations, but it was also applying them to all the oil it traded. This latter was a *massive* breakaway from the rest of the industry, given that Wilmar trades some 45% of the global palm oil supplies.

Two days later I was in Jakarta, and Michael Bachelard, an Australian journalist and colleague, asked 'How did it happen?' It took time for me to explain how the company's process had unfolded. But what I focused on as the pivotal moment in the journey was a small piece of philosophy, a cartoon by Australian artist Michael Leunig, I had sent to Wilmar's Chairman. It had been, I believed, crucial in helping get the decision over the line.

"At the top of the tallest building in the world . . . sat the saddest man in the world and inside the man was the loneliest heart in the world and inside the heart was the deepest pit in the world and at the bottom of the pit was the blackest mud in the world and

in the mud lay the lightest, loveliest, tenderest, most beautiful happy angel in the universe. So things weren't so bad, after all. 🙮
'AT THE TOP', BY MICHAEL LEUNIG

Poems? Cartoons? Michael subsequently published an article on the change process, describing the use of poetry, cartoons and philosophy as an 'unusual method'. He's right. It's highly unusual in the normal business world of facts, figures, tick-boxes and command and control. It's hugely effective because it touches people in a much deeper, more personal way.

The beauty of VT-TV, a Values-based approach, is that it creates so much more room for broad exploration. It helps people open up very quickly to wide discussion. Why? Because it doesn't force someone else's tick-boxes and agendas on people. Instead it speaks to *their* hearts and souls, emotions and fundamental belief systems. It pushes *them* to express what *they* truly believe, to find a path to the breakaway, the Angel within. To do so it can use poetry, art, music, philosophy, whimsy. It can speak of love, tender things.

We humans have an inherent capacity for good. Think what we might be able to achieve if we just set those Angels within us free. My experience tells me that when we bring that good thing to the surface, look out! It has incredible, unstoppable power to change how whole industries operate and how we engage with one another to effect change. We've got to stop taking false cures and deal with what's inside us honestly, openly and urgently.

For me, two events put the final nails in the certification coffin, and I want to share them with you.

I turned 50 last year and decided my family should have chooks again.[4] My youngest bloke and I bought a fine chook pen at the store of a TFT member. I purchased it thinking it was made from FSC certified fir. But I had some concerns because it had been produced in China, so I asked my TFT colleague there to do some digging. What he found were all the issues with certification I've raised here – a factory with a valid FSC COC certificate, but a wood supplier that was *not* FSC-certified, a recent audit by the FSC certification body that found everything in order because it had no idea about the status of the upstream wood supplier. My magnificent new chook pen appeared to have been falsely labelled as FSC wood! But wait! Some months later, my TFT China colleagues were called by the CB to be told that actually everything is OK – 'we've found the documents!' Should I still be concerned? This is why I believe so passionately in independent Verification!

At this same time a human rights NGO issued a report on the abuse of migrant workers in the palm oil industry. Among other things companies were holding workers' identity documents and passports, having them sign contracts they didn't understand and paying wages below the statutory minimum. The plantations studied for the report were all RSPO and ISCC certified.[5] When the report came out, RSPO's weak response included this on the living wage issue: 'We never said we guarantee it, only minimum wage.'

VT-TV brings about real change because it is based on the power and passion of the breakaway, on that inherent, internal desire to do the right thing. It is about breaking the shackles of control and *freeing people* from ticking someone else's boxes or being audited against someone else's standard. It's about opening the heart to the birds, to mystery, messages of poetry, love, art, spirituality, religion, to so many possibilities. We're free to dream of a better future, to do the right thing. Ideas form, strategies are tested, two steps forward, three steps back, but slowly a path emerges amid the gloom. As we're seeing across a wide range of sectors, VT-TV works. Once started, progress happens.

The start is the hardest part. The task seems horrendously daunting, the challenges epic. There's a sense you're too insignificant to matter, so why bother, or you decide it is someone else's responsibility or, most sadly of all, that someone else will fix it and you can carry on until then. Here a ball of confused fishing line offers a valuable lesson. If we calmly tease out the entanglement rather than pulling tightly on the two ends, we untangle it in less time and with less angst than we anticipated. Even better, it was fun.

For too long we have believed that we can use technological prowess to control all the messiness we create. Falling into that hole was our chapter 1. Our chapter 2 was relying on chemicals and destructive farming practices when we needed to increase food production. Chapter 3 might have been the first UN Rio Earth Summit, when we finally admitted the mess was our fault and we needed to do something about it. Certification was, perhaps, chapter 4: under the label of sustainability we sought to walk around the holes of over-exploitation, destroyed livelihoods, species loss, etc., but all the while kept to the same street and continued falling into the holes.

I maintain that only such processes as VT-TV – beautiful, poetic, spiritual, soulful – can help us, as a species, extricate ourselves from the trouble we're in, and to live more in balance with ourselves as a part of nature. Working together with nature, we can move toward chapter 5. We won't get there because we aren't yet dealing with the overriding driver of this mess – over-consumption. Supplying too much stuff to too many people is killing the planet. As in the case of my chook pen, certification's ultimate failure is that it tells us we're good to go with respect to consumption when clearly we're not. Although VT-TV itself isn't yet there, my own experience tells me it is moving us along a new and proper path. Personally, I now strive to keep my consumption as low as possible, paying more attention, for example, to how electricity reaches my home and being open to looking deeply into issues I've hardly touched in the past.

To conclude . . .

I believe we humans have good inside us, our Angels, and that it is time to break away from our addiction to certification, from all the complex, controlling systems we've built. We need to set ourselves free and, with passion, to do the right thing. We need to find tools that connect us with our Angel. If we do this together, we might reach chapter 5.

Although VT-TV is one way to do that, this is a time for people to propose other ideas on how to set our Angels free. So onward. Let yourselves go, *su corragio*. As with our tangled fishing line, it might even be fun. Apply Ockham's Razor principle: simpler theories are preferable to more complex ones. We need everyone's imagination!

I finish with another small but inspiring quote from a wonderful story by Jean Giono called *The Man Who Planted Hope and Grew Happiness* (1954):

> **"When I reminded myself that all this was the work of the hand and soul of one man with no mechanical help it seemed to me that men could be as effective as god in tasks other than destruction."**

References

Beckett, S. 1954. *Waiting for Godot* (New York: Grove Press).

Caldwell, L.K. 1990. *Between Two Worlds: Science, the Environmental Movement and Policy Choice* (Cambridge: Cambridge University Press).

Giono, J. 1981 [1954]. *The Man Who Planted Hope and Grew Happiness*, 7th printing (Brooksville, ME: Friends of Nature).

Leunig, M. 1990 *A Common Prayer* (New York: HarperCollins Publishers).

Nelson, P. 1977. 'Autobiography in Five Short Chapters'. In *There's a Hole in My Sidewalk: The Romance of Self-Discovery* (Hillsboro, OR: Popular Library, Beyond Words Publishing).

Pirsig, R.M. 1974. *Zen and the Art of Motorcycle Maintenance* (New York: HarperCollins Publishers).

Sheehan, N. 1988. *A Bright Shining Lie* (New York: Vintage Books).

Notes

1. 'Cube' by Michael Leunig

2. American philosopher and systems scientist C. West Churchman coined the term 'wicked problem' in the late 1970s. He used it to describe those challenges that are complex, ill-defined, ambiguous and associated with strong moral issues set in a highly dynamic context – they won't keep still, no one is truly in command and no plan can possibly be set in advance to solve them. The only way to tackle them is to dive straight into the complexity, engage with all the parts of the system and work your way forward, tackling all the moving and dynamic issues as you go. The usual structured and command/control approaches don't solve wicked problems – doing so requires adaptive leadership, the willingness to get messy and seeing things differently.

3. For an explanation of first, second and third party verification, please see: http://www.fao.org/docrep/006/y5136e/y5136e07.htm

4. A 'chook' is what we Australians call a chicken. Not sure why . . .

5. International Sustainability & Carbon Certification: http://www.iscc-system. org/en/

....